Summary

MW00933767

of

Where the Crawdads Sing

By

Dalia Owens

Book Nerd

Our Free Gift to You

We would like to thank you for being a fan and for reading this series with two free books on affirmations and procrastination. Download your free ebooks now:

https://www.subscribepage.com/2books

Sincerely,

The Book Nerd Team

Table of Contents

This is an unofficial summary & analysis of Delia Owens' *Where the Crawdads Sing*. This summary is designed to enrich your reading experience. Buy the original book here:
https://www.amazon.com/Where-Crawdads-Sing-Delia-Owens-ebook/dp/B078GD3DRG/

Prologue of Where the Crawdads Sing

This chapter is set in 1969 and depicts the difference between a swamp and a marsh. On October 30th of that year a body was found in the swamp, and it was the body of someone named Chase Andrews. Swamps are dark while marshes are light. The dead body was spotted by two boys on bikes who saw a denim jacket on the body.

Chapter One Summary of Where the Crawdads Sing

The year is 1952. We are introduced to a character named Kya who is six years old and lives with her mom, dad, and siblings in a shack. It's August, and the setting appears to be near a marsh. Kya hears the door slam and is surprised because she knows her mother doesn't slam doors. She saw her mom walking away when she came to the porch. The mom was wearing high heeled, fake alligator skin shoes. Her mom was unsteady in high heels and she usually brought meat when she came home. Kya has five sibling, and she is the youngest. Jodie is Kya's eleven year old brother, and he thinks their mom will be back soon but Kya isn't so sure because she has a blue briefcase and is wearing alligator patterned shoes. The marsh was connected to a shoreline and is at the coast of North Carolina. The marsh was settled by people who escaped the law, diseases, taxes, and slavery. It was also settled by sailors and renegades. The marsh is described as a net which captured all kinds of people and wildlife. There was plenty of shellfish and wildlife to eat so one would not starve. No one wanted to be on this land nor cared about it because it was considered to be a wasteland.

The mother didn't come back that day, and Kya's two sisters made supper. Kya is tall, tan, and skinny. She has black hair. Kya greeted her mother in the morning. Kya's father was either silent or loud most of the time. Kya noticed a bruise on her mom's forehead which she covered with a scarf.

The next morning, Kya's mom wasn't there and she played sword fighting with her brother near the woods. Kya's mom never came home that day.

Chapter Two Summary of Where the Crawdads Sings

Kya's older brothers and sisters grew distant too, and one day they left after their dad's persistent fits of rage. Jodie, Kya's brother, made breakfast one day like mom used to cook it, and he and Kya ate it before dad woke up. They decided to go to the marsh after breakfast, but dad started hollering at them. Jodie said that they can run and hide near the moss.

One day Jodie told Kya that he will be leaving home and that when she gets older she'll understand. Kya wanted to beg him to stay, but the words didn't come out of her mouth. Jodie taught Kya how to hide in the bushes in case anything goes wrong. Kya got hungry. She cooked for herself and realized her dad wasn't home. She was alone home at night for the first time. Dad wasn't home for three days. Dad finally came home on the fourth day with a bottle. He asked Kya where everyone went, and she said she doesn't know. Kya smelled smoke and found out that dad was burning all of Mom's things in the yard. She tried to stop her dad. Kya watched all her Mom's things burn down. Kya left the shack before her Dad did each morning and lived mostly in the woods. She came home only to sleep near the porch.

Dad had served in the Second World War. His femur was shattered, and he was only earning a small disability check. The week after Jodie was gone, Dad gave Kya a dollar with some change for food. Jodie ~~Kya~~ walked to the market for four miles for the first time on her own. The Everglades were in the background. There were several shops on the two main streets. The three intersections of this town were the Atlantic Ocean, Main Street, and Broad Street. The buildings were over two hundred years old and had not been maintained. Kya was barefooted and wore overalls; she was headed to Piggly Wiggly to buy groceries. Three boys on bikes rode past her, and they appeared to be troublemakers since they almost crashed into someone. A landowner named Miss Pansy Price called out to Chase Andrews and the three boys. Chase apologized and told Miss Pansy that he didn't see her due to the girl here (he was referring to Kya). Miss Pansy told the boys to help Miss Arial, their former second grade teacher, with her groceries. Chase was a dark haired, tan boy who had the hottest red bike because his parents owned the auto store. When Kya got her groceries she walked up the lady at the checkout register, Mrs. Singletary, and when asked where her mom is, she lied and said that Mom is doing chores. Kya bought grit and ran home after she was a reasonable distance away from the store. Kya didn't really know how to cook grit and messed up the meal so she found some more turnips in the garden. The grit would lump up, but she figured out how to cook it. Kya rarely spoke to her father; they lived separate lives and would not run into each other for days. Kya cooked, cleaned, and did the laundry to maintain their shack clean because she was waiting for Mom to return. She cleaned up after Dad too. Kya believed her birthday was in the fall, and she spent the day feeding grit to the seagulls.

Chapter Three Summary of Where the Crawdads Sings

The year is 1969 again. This chapter is about Chase. The sound of crows was audible. Two blond boys, both aged ten, named Benji Mason and Steve Long find the body of Chase Andrew under the fire tower of the swamp. The boys recognize him and decide to ride their bikes to Main street as fast as they could. They were uneasy staying at the swamp. They went straight to Sheriff Ed Jackson, and the sheriff asked them to show him the body. Dr. Vern Murphy, the town physician, also went to see the body. The crows flew away when Ed and Dr. Murphy went to see the body. The doctor examined the body and said Chase has been dead for about ten hours. One of then thought that Chase fell off from the fire tower and died. The two men can't figure out why no one discovered the body earlier since people come in packs to this area. Chase's footprints were not found at the scene which confused the doctor and the sheriff.

Chapter Four Summary of Where the Crawdads Sings

The year is 1952 once again, and this chapter is about Kya.

Kya watched a few people arrive by car near her shack and was scared because no one ever comes to her house. They knocked on her door and said there are truancy officers and are here to take Catherine Clark to school. Kya didn't know how to talk to kids and wanted to learn to read. The truancy officers said she would get a free meal in school. Mrs. Culpepper said she wants to take her to school. Kya had to wear a dress or skirt to school because she is a girl. The white kids and kids of color went to two separate schools. The two schools were in Barkley Cove; the school for whites was in Main and the school for black kids was in Colored Town. They put Kya in second grade randomly. Some kids wore shoes but others were barefooted. Mrs. Arial became her second grade teacher; the same one those three boys assisted with groceries. Kya's full name is Catherine Danielle Clark; that's what she said to the class. Kya learned phonics and at eleven o'clock got breakfast at school. She got chicken pie and banana pudding, and sat at a table by herself. She recognized the three boys from her trip to the market, but they all ignored her. Kya noticed a few blond girls with full skirts. Kya stayed quiet in class because she didn't want classmates to laugh at her. The blond girls make fun of Kya at the end of the day, and the bus drops her off in the woods. She had to run home and went near the ocean, and the gulls appeared to sing. Kya wished she could take the bird with her and have them sleep next to her. For a few weeks, the truancy officers came to pick up Kya, but she ran away from them and left confusing footprints behind as her brother taught her. Then one day, no one came anymore and Kya never went to school. Kya believed she could learn by collecting shells and bird watching. A few weeks later Kya, found a nail in her right foot and yanked it out. It appeared that her Dad was not home. Kya knew she had to get a tetanus shot within two days of stepping on a lockjaw; at least that's what her brother told her at one point. Kya decided to soak her foot in brine because she didn't know where to get a shot. Dad seemed to be away playing poker and drinking whiskey. Kya wondered if she would die from her punctured foot, but she was okay. She woke up in the morning to doves in the oak trees.

Her Dad wasn't home for a week and she had to survive on eating saltines with Crisco. Her foot almost healed completely by the eighth day. She went to the pool two times a day. Mom's favorite food was scrambled eggs for breakfast. She had her own hens until Kya accidentally released them. Cornbread fritters with tomatoes were also added to the eggs.

A few months passed and it was winter. The earth, especially the marsh became a mother to Kya. (The earth being Mom is a metaphor)

Chapter Five Summary of Where the Crawdads Sings

The year is 1969 again.

Sheriff Jackson says that Chase's family doesn't know yet that he's dead. Ed told the three boys not to go anywhere while the doctor said he would go and inform Chase's family. A deputy named Joe Purdue shows up and can't believe Chase is dead. He was a great quarterback. The deputy looks for evidence. The driver took the body away. The two boys were told to go home by Ed the sheriff. Ed found it strange that the grate wasn't closed on the stairs of the fire tower which means someone could fall down sixty feet; Ed suspects that someone left the grate open on purpose. Ed thinks that someone made it look like Chase fell down on his own, but he isn't sure if there's foul play at this point. Joe and Ed take fingerprints. Joe says that Chase went around before he was married and even after he was married so there may be a few people who wanted him dead. Joe doesn't think Chase was up in the tower with a stranger.

Chapter Six Summary of Where the Crawdads Sings

It's 1952. Dad came to the kitchen dressed formally and was leaving for Asheville. He told Kya he would be gone for up to four days. He wanted to discuss his disability payments with the army. Kya wasn't sure if her dad was going to leave her, and he never usually tells her where he's going so she was surprised. He waved goodbye at her dismissively which is more than Mom had done when she left. Kya was tempted to use Dad's boat but knew she would get in trouble if she did. She checked how much gas the boat had by dipping a reed into the gas tank and figured it was enough for a short ride. She was only seven at this time. She steered the boat for a hundred yard and heard birds cawing. She recalled her brother's advice on using the boat several times during her trip. She drifted through estuaries and lagoons. There were no people or boat where she was, and she started to look like a swamp child. She passed by a boy in a red baseball cap on a boat, and then she wanted to go home. She got lost. She stood there in her boat in the middle of the water for a while and decided she had no choice but to try and find the boy in the cap so she can ask him for directions. She started to cry when telling the boy she's lost. She was surprised he knew her brother and her name. A storm was coming and the boy guided Kya to her home by having her follow his boat. She realized where she got lost. He told her his name is Tate. Kya realized she used up a lot of gas and needed to refill the tank before her dad got back. Kya realized she felt so calm near the boy and she wasn't close to him. She knew she needed him and his boat; she felt no emotional pain during this day for the first time ever since Mom and her brother left.

Tate Walked went to visit his father. Everyone called his dad Scupper. Scupper's family had Scottish ancestry. Tate made hamburgers with his mom and sister. Scupper asks Tate how school is going. Scupper tells Tate that real men read poetry, cry, feel opera, and defend women. Tate began to read a poem. Tate found a poem which reminded him of Kya.

Chapter Seven Summary of Where the Crawdads Sings

The year is still 1952.Kya sat on the porch and thought about how few people she talked to. Kya avoid Mrs. Singletary at the Piggly Wiggly because she keeps asking her questions about her Mom. Kya talks even less to people than before but likes talking to gulls. Her family was once called swamp trash by someone. Dad used the boat to fish and doesn't have a car. Kya wished she could borrow the boat from her Dad, but doesn't know what she would trade him for it. Kya did a lot of cooking and cleaning. She was starting to forget what her brothers looked like. Kya bought gas from Sing Oil station and bought groceries. She filled the boat with gas and scrubbed it with wet sand when she got home. Kya was starting to get worried that her father wasn't coming home, but on the evening of the fourth day he finally showed up. Her Dad finally saw the hot food she prepared on the table and thanked her. The two ate quietly. Dad asked Kya for more food. Kya said there's plenty left and filled his plate. Kya felt like she needed to talk to someone which is why she needed her Dad around. She asked him if she can go fishing with him sometime. Her Dad decided to take her fishing. Kya got the worms as her dad told her and secretly hoped she wouldn't catch a fish. She did catch one and her Dad cheered like she's never heard him cheer before. The next day, Kya went fishing with her Dad again. He made fried fish supper. Dad gave Kya his World War II knapsack so she could store the feathers and hummingbird nest she collected. Kya realized her Dad had never given her anything before.

Kya and her Dad went to the estuary or creek every warm day in the spring and winter. Kya kept scanning the water for that boy she saw, and one day she found him in the same place she met him before while she was in the boat with her Dad. She waved her hand at him, and Dad told her to be careful because there's too much white trash in this area. She didn't look at the boy again but didn't want him to think of her as unfriendly. Dad was very knowledgeable about how to navigate the marsh. He told he about goose season, fishing, and the weather. One day, Dad mentioned that his parents weren't always poor. They used to have tobacco fields and cotton fields until the depression happened. Then all that was left were debts. Kya didn't even know she had a grandma; she really wanted to know what happened to all her family members but was afraid to ask Dad. Kya knew that her mom used to wear dressed bought at stores before she moved to the shack, but Dad burned everything in that fire. Dad mentioned to Kya that he will take her to see Ashville one day to show her the land that should have been hers. Dad caught a fish and called Kya "hon" which surprised her.

Chapter Eight Summary of Where the Crawdads Sings

The year is 1969.

Sheriff Ed and Deputy Joe brought in the parents and widow of Chase so they can pay their condolences and see his body on a steel table. Ed's office was full of erosion and mold. Joe had the lab results back from the crime scene and found negative data. They knew Chase died on October 29th or 30th, but no fingerprints were found. From the data, there were no footprints found of anyone. So it wasn't clear that Chase walked up the stairs at all. Ed and Joe were now convinced that Chase was killed. The two stopped at Barkley Cove Diner, and the air smelled like cooked food. Mr. Lane from Sing Oil thought that Lamar Sands killed Chase because him wife cheated with Chase. Ed and Joe decide to take their food to-go because they don't want to hear diners speculate about who killed Chase. Miss Pansy Price thought it was the woman who lives on the marsh who killed him.

Chapter Nine Summary of Where the Crawdads Sings

It's 1953.

Kya's boat moved towards the Marina Gas Station. It was owned by a guy named Jumpin' who had this named because he always sprung up to help people. Dad introduced Kya to the gas station owner and asked him to fill the tank. Jumpin' was also called Mister Jake. Dad then took Kya to Barkley Cove Diner, and she had never been to the restaurant before. People at the restaurant stared at Kya and one said that she probably can't read the sign that says that wearing shoes and a shirt is required here. Kya never wore shoes. Kya and Dad sat at a small table and ordered a lot of food. Kya was stuffed. Kya took her leftover food and saltines when she left the restaurant. A little girl said "hi" to her and reached out to Kya until Mrs. Teresa White, the mother, told her to get away. Barkley Cove had four churches for whites and three for blacks. People took religion seriously in this town. Teresa White told her little daughter not to touch Kya because she was dirty. She noticed how long the mother and little girl stared into each other's eyes. Dad told her they had to go because of the tide. Dad sill left for many days at times, but when he came home he would actually talk with Kya and play games. Kya though her Mom may come back because she's been gone since last summer. Dad used to beat up his family when he was drunk, so maybe that's why they all left. Kya didn't know why her family fought so much. Her mother used to paint with watercolors and oils.

Kya found a letter from her mom in the mailbox in September. She left the letter where Dad can see it, but found that he burned the letter and left by boat. Kya didn't know how to read so she could only read her Mom's name. Kya picked up the ashes of the letter and stored them in a box. She knew Dad would never tell her where Mom went.

Dad finally came back home after a few days and was drunk again. He told Kya that Mom isn't coming back, but she didn't believe him. Dad didn't take Kya fishing again. Kya wanted to pray but didn't know how to. She thought life was better with all the shouting than it is now. When she looked at Mom's garden, she decided that God wasn't going to come here in any case.

Chapter Ten Summary of Where the Crawdads Sings

It's 1969.

The sheriff went to investigate the area around the fire tower but only found animal tracks. Ed and Joe went to the bay but only found prints created by animals and plants. The bay was covered by shells and crustacean parts, Shells are good at keeping secrets.

Chapter Eleven Summary of Where the Crawdads Sings

It's 1956.It's winter time, and Dad barely came home at all. Kya wondered if Dad was beat up in a poker game or fell down after getting drunk. She decided her Dad is gone, but she couldn't mourn him like she mourned Mom. Kya would have to pretend to everyone that Dad was still around or authorities would take her away. Kya didn't have much money left and she was stretching it as far as possible. Her Dad left on foot since the boat was still here. Kya pretended to read the fairy-tales. She still couldn't read at age ten. Her kerosene lamp ran out of kerosene, and she didn't know what to do. She found a candle and lit it up. The next morning, Kya collected mussels like her Mom taught her. She decided that the marsh is her family. She decided to go to Jumpin's Gas and Bait and was able to trade the mussels for some cash and gas. She bought a candle, matches, and grit at Jumpin's shop with the money she just made. Kya asked how much mussels he buys per week and he told her forty pounds every few days. But Kya had competitors who also sold mussels to Jumpin'. Kya felt like a grown-up because she purchased her own supplies. Kya gathered up mussels at night and even picked up some oysters. She slept close to Jumpin's store so she can get to him first in the morning. Her money was more reliable than the money her Dad used to give her on Mondays. She no longer went to the Piggly Wiggly store because Mrs. Singletary questioned why she wasn't at school. Kya got what she needed at Jumpin's store.

Chapter Twelve Summary of Where the Crawdads Sings

Kya would listen for people outside her shack. She seemed lonely. She kept looking for Tate, the boy who helped her find her way home once. One day, Kya saw Tate in the distance and recognized him right away by his blond curls. She watched Tate as if she was watching a heron. She continued to collect shells and feathers. She wore the clothes of her old siblings because hers were worn out. One day, Kya rode her boat to Point Beach. She saw several boys and girls on the beach and recognized Chase Andrews. She found their voices pleasant and seemed to want to talk to the girls. She watched the kids while hiding from them and wondered what it would be like to have friends. Kya was unable to sell her mussels this week to Jumpin' because she lost to her competitors and now had no money left. Kya had another idea; she decided to go fishing and cooked smoked fish. She offered them to Jumpin' the next day, and he decided to get them from her on consignment. Jumpin' lived in Colored Town and had a real house instead of just a shack. His wife, Mabel, offered to support Kya in some way and trade with her for things she needed. When Kya went to Jumpin' the next day, she met his wife, Mabel. Mabel said she knows of families who will give her clothes for her smoked fish. Kya wanted gas and Mabel said they'll give her some because they know she's running low. Mabel took Kya's measurements so she can bring her clothes and shoes. Mabel explained to Kya how to garden. When Kya got home, she began to hoe the soil and found her mom's barrette.

When Kya got to Jumpin' the next day, he presented her with two boxes full of goods. Kya said that these goods are worth a whole month of fish. She got clothes and food. She put on the lace blouse right away and rode her boat home.

Chapter Thirteen Summary of Where the Crawdads Sings

The year is 1960.
Kya is now fourteen. Kya was finally able to wear Mom's pink and green sundress. Kya went fishing. Crows are bad at keeping secrets so Kya knew something was up when they kept making noise. She saw a boy older than she was rushing through the woods. The boy saw her, and Kya hid. Kya didn't catch any fish that day because she was hiding from the boy. Kya saw the feather of the great blue heron stuck in a stump, and she didn't know how it got there. Kya thought the boy put the feather there, so she decided to go home and lock the door. She retrieved the feather at dawn. The next morning after that, she found a white feather in the stump. Kya still couldn't read. Kya didn't find any more feathers on that stump for more than a week. Then Kya found a Turkey feather on the stump. Kya saw a bird attacking one of its own weak birds so that it wouldn't attract predators to the heard about a year ago. Kya shooed them away. The hen was dead after being attacked by its own flock of hens. A group of five teenage boys tried to break down her door but didn't. They called her names like Marsh Girl and laughed at her; this reminded her of the turkey incident.

Chapter Fourteen Summary of Where the Crawdads Sings

The year is 1969.

Joe tells Ed that he has more data on Chase Andrew's case. Injuries were found on Chase's body, and he hit his head on the beam as he was falling down. This new lab result showed that Chase died where he was found. He died because of the impact of the fall on his head and spinal cord. Ed concluded that someone erased all the fingerprints and footprints. His jacket was filled with strange fibers.

Chapter Fifteen Summary of Where the Crawdads Sings

The year is 1960.
Kya decides to leave eagle feather for the mysterious person leaving her feathers. She believed a person who liked birds could be harmful. Kya cut eight inches off her hair. She decided to use her Mom's old makeup that she found at home. Kya found the nail polish her mom once used. Mom took the girls on the boat one day. When Kya got to the oak clearing the next day, she found a feather and a milk carton. Inside the carton were vegetables and a boat spark plug. She saw a letter in the carton but couldn't read it. Kya filled her bags with mussels by dawn. She then went to the oak clearing to leave her feather and saw the boy who was leaving her feathers. It was Tate! Tate told her not to run. Tate thought Kya was strikingly pretty. Kya admitted to him that she can't read his note. Tate paraphrased what he had written to her. Kya thanked her for the supplies he brought her, the spark plug and seeds. Tate started to walk away because he realized Kya wasn't going to say anything else. Before he left, he told her that he could teach her how to read.

Chapter Sixteen Summary of Where the Crawdads Sings

It's 1960.Kya decided to get to Jumpin's house even though she didn't know exactly where it was. Kya decided she was lonely and wanted to talk to Mabel. She took blackberry jam for the couple. Kya witnessed some white boys throwing rocks at Jumpin' and calling him names. Kya wacked one of the boys with her jar bag, and he fell on his face. The other one ran off. The following day, Tate decided to go visit Kya to teach her how to read. Tate was teaching her the alphabet and tried to teach her to spell words she already knew. Tate came over to Kya's place a few times a week when he wasn't working with his dad. Kya found out that Tate live with his Dad in Barkley Cove. She wanted to reach out and touch his hand, but her fingers wouldn't let her. Kya loved practicing her reading and writing on her own at night. Kya didn't know why Tate was treating her, poor white trash so nicely. Kya was able to write out all of her collections specimens now that she knew how to write. Kya asked Tate what the next number after twenty-nine is, and he didn't want to shame her. Kya tried to read anything she could get her hands on. One day, she found her family's names and birthdates in the family Bible. She was ashamed that she had forgotten their names. Kya now knew her parents' proper names. Her mom was from New Orleans. The bank took the Clarks' land during the depression, and Jake, her Dad, ended up working on the tobacco fields with the slaves. Jake left with family heirlooms one day and took his family's heirlooms. He went to New Orleans where he met Maria, Kya's mother. Jake took a job at the shoe factory which was owned by Maria's father because Jake's family was already broke at this time. The father of Maria wanted Jake to work his way up like the rest of the employees. Jake wanted to finish high school but ended up being drunk too often and played poker. Maria wanted him to stop drinking, but he didn't. They had a lot of babies, and Jake only got promoted once. There was a war with Germany, and Jake was in France when a mortar exploded and shattered his left leg. Many thought Jake was a hero because people thought he was trying to rescue someone when the mortar exploded, but Jake was just hiding. Jake received a medal and was sent home on medical discharge. Jake didn't want to work at the shoe factory in New Orleans, so he sold Maria's valuables and moved the family to North Carolina. Jake moved the family to a cabin with no rent. Maria was sad after living there for a while because their situation didn't improve, and Jake never finished high school. Jake drank and played poker all the time, and Maria did the best she could to provide a good home. She enrolled her children at school, but some of them skipped class. Jake once took Maria on a boat ride and she got pregnant with Catherine who was called Kya because that's what she called herself as a toddler. Sometimes Jake wanted to finish school when he sobered up.

Chapter Seventeen Summary of Where the Crawdads Sings

The year is 1960.

Jumpin' told Kya that some men came looking for her and asking where she went to school and where her parents were. Jumpin' said he did his best to put them off. Kya decided that she may need to go into hiding for a while. When Tate came over, Kya asked to meet him elsewhere. She said Social Services were looking for her. Tate says that she needs to be hidden where the crawdads sing; by this, he means in the wild. Kya thought of an abandoned cabin she knew and got on Tate's boat to show him where it is. When they got to the cabin, Tate said that he hopes she doesn't stay at this place long since it's dilapidated. She says she has to go into hiding for a while. Tate says that it would be good for her to go to school so that they don't keep looking for her. Kya says she's too old for school and that she'd rather live on the marsh than go to a foster home. Tate read books with Kya in the summer and she read books about nature which she would have never read at school.

Kya collected firewood for winter. She had Tate brought the mussels and fish to Jumpin'. Tate read a poem to Kya and she started making up her own poems. She took out her mom's poetry book and read her favorite poems. Kya couldn't understand the message of the poems clearly, but she knew they had a powerful message. Tate couldn't visit Kya as much during his senior year of high school. They met near her shack instead of near the abandoned cabin. Kya invited Tate to sit near her kitchen stove for the first time. Tate didn't have time to visit as much because he was working with his Dad. Kya read a love novel on her Mom's bookshelf.

Mabel greeted Kya, and Jumpin' filled her tank. Mabel had given Kya the most beautiful peach colored dress, prettier than her Mom's dresses. She also got a white bra.

Kya got a stomach ache a few weeks later just as Tate came to see her. Tate asked her if her stomachache felt different than others she'd gotten. She said it was different, and he told her it might be something that's natural for girls her age. Tate reminded her of the pamphlet he brought her, and Kya was embarrassed for growing up right in front of a boy. She didn't know how much blood she would lose. Tate couldn't look at her and asked if she could get herself home. Tate said he would follow behind her just to make sure she got home safely.

The next day, Kya went to see Mabel urgently. She only saw Jumpin' and he had to leave his gas station for a while to go get his wife. Mabel came in Kya's boat and explained to her what a period is and brought her some stuff.

The next day Tate came to visit Kya, but she was too embraced and hid from him because he knew something very personal about her. Tate brought small cakes. Kya ate the cakes but still couldn't look at Tate. The two started reading a new book.

Autumn was almost here, and Kya finally got the nerve to ask Tate why he was so nice to her. Tate says he likes that Kya values the marsh, and he doesn't have a girlfriend. Tate had some mixed feeling for Kya which he didn't mention to her. He saw her as a lost sister and an attractive girl at the same time. Kya asked Tate where his mom is, and he said she and his sister died in a car accident in Asheville. Kya apologized for his loss and told him that her mom walked out on her one day. Tate feels like his mom and sister died because they went out to get a bike for him the day they got hit by a car. The wind blew off tons of leaves off a sycamore tree, and Tate suggested they catch as many leaves as possible before they fall to the ground. The two bumped into each other, and Tate kissed her. The next moment was awkward and then Kya asked him if she was his girlfriend. Kya's heart was beating fast. Tate at first said she was too young to be his girlfriend, but then agreed. They kissed again. Kya felt complete for the first time in her life.

Chapter Eighteen Summary of Where the Crawdads Sings

Kya and Tate spent time at the beach. The next day, he brought a picnic basket. It was a birthday gift for Kya; she turned fifteen. Inside the box was a cake and presents. Tate said he found out about her birthday from the family Bible when she asked him about it. He gave her a magnifying glass, a hair clip, and a painting set.

Tate was painting a boat with Scupper. Tate got paid while working for Scupper. Tate never mentioned Kya to his Dad. Scupper took Tate to a restaurant after work because they were both too tired to cook a meal for themselves. Scupper asks Tate if he has any plans to take a girl to the big dance at his school, and Tate says he doesn't like any of the girls at his school. Then his dad says there's a rumor going around that he's seeing the swamp girl, and he says she must be a nice girl but warms Tate not to start a family at an early age. Tate says that she's pure unlike the girls at his school. His dad says not to get upset at him because it's his job as a parent to warn him of certain things. Dad says how proud he is of Tate and his college acceptance.

Tate sometimes went to see Kya but didn't stay long. The two held hands and kissed. He really wanted to touch her, but he was also very protective of her. Tate would bring Kya books, and she was a good enough reader to read any book now. She learned a lot about biology. She looked for a biological explanations for why mothers leave their kids.

One day in the winter, Tate brought Kya a gift, and she didn't realize it was Christmas. The gift was a dictionary and a pelican feather. When Tate left, Kya got angry at herself for not getting a gift for her loved one. A few days later, Kya wore the peach dress Mabel gave her and waited for Tate to bring the Turkey dinner. They both prepared the dinner and Tate offered to clean up but ended up holding Kya as she was washing something. She leaned on him.

The winter turned to spring soon enough. They saw a white bullfrog while on a walk one day. Then things got more intimate and Tate started to explore her. Tate the apologized to Kya for treating her so sexually, but Kya said she liked it and tried to push him towards her. Tate said she's too young, and he's four years older. He said they should wait.

In May Tate mentioned that he's going away to Chapel Hill College. Tate said he's leaving for the summer because he got a job at a biology lab at his college. Kya was upset by this even though Tate promised to visit. She ran off into the woods.

A week later, Tate came to visit Kya and told her that he has to skip his high school graduation because his job was starting very soon. At first Kya couldn't speak, but then told Tate she would miss him. Tate promises to come back by the 4th of July. Kya says that he might get busy with life and college girls, but Tate didn't think so. Tate gave Kya a long goodbye kiss.

Chapter Nineteen Summary of Where the Crawdads Sings

The year is 1969.
The deputy went to Sheriff Ed's office and brought donuts and coffee. The deputy brought a second lab report, and said Chase did something at the marsh. Deputy Joe said Chase would go to the marsh by himself a lot, and he believed he may have gotten involved with some drug thug. The sheriff said they need to learn more about his life. Chase's mom said that the shell necklace he wore is a clue of some kind. Chase's mom was supposed to come to the office to discuss the necklace soon.

Chapter Twenty Summary of Where the Crawdads Sings

The year is 1961.
On July 4th Kya waited on the lagoon for Tate in her peach chiffon dress. Tate didn't show up, and she swam in the water at night. After the second day, Kya no longer expected Tate to show up. Kya watched as a female firefly ate a male firefly of a different species after confusing him with her flashing signals. Kya didn't think it was evil; it was just how life went even if there are sacrifices. There is no right or wrong in biology. The following day, Kya went to the lagoon to wait for Tate and screamed out his name.

Chapter Twenty-One Summary of Where the Crawdads Sings

It's 1961.

Kya didn't leave her bed for three days. None of the birds outside got her out of bed either. She wondered why everyone she loved always left her. She didn't want to love or trust anyone after Tate. The sun shone in her face, and she saw a hawk. She got up to make grit and went to feed gulls. The birds circled around her, and she was content even though there were tears on her face. Kya stayed home for a month. Kya saw the Cooper's hawk again and decided to go to the marsh. She felt abandoned by Tate, but was curious about what college must be like. She collected more natural specimens but grew lonelier. Life was back to normal by August. She wanted to connect with people again. A few years went by.

Part 2: On the Swamp

Chapter Twenty-Two Summary of Where the Crawdads Sings

Kya was nineteen now and watched a group of young adults on Point Beach. It was the same group of friends she'd seen several times. Sometimes this group of friends made fun of Kya, and she though that it's significant that they're still together after all these years. Mabel told Kya she needs some girlfriends because they stick around forever. Kya felt even lonelier when she watched them. Chase Andrews was part of that friend group, and Kya watched him. Chase's ball fell where Kya was hiding, and he noticed her. Chase passed the ball to his friends and then looked Kya in the eyes. He had black hair and blue eyes. Chase got back to his friends while Kya followed the group around, spying on them. Kya kept going back to the beach each day to look for Chase. Kya lay on the beach one day after staring at Chase and waits for a wave to come to her. Kya feels like the ocean held her and that she's not alone. Kya ran into Chase at Jumpin's shop while he was refilling crates. Chase invited Kya to a picnic on his boat. Kya agreed to go. Kya refilled her tank and recited poetry on her way back home.

Tate came to visit Kya in July, but she didn't know it. It turns out that Dr. Blum, Tate's professor invited Tate to a bird watching expedition during the Fourth of July weekend. He went see her two weeks later and watched her observing nature. Then he heard a boat approach and was startled to see how scared of it Kya was. It was just a fisherman, but Tate was turned off by Kya's reaction so he decided to leave without even telling her that he's here to see her. Tate had to choose either Kya or everything else in his life. He choose everything else but felt terrible for not saying goodbye to her.

Chapter Twenty-Three Summary of Where the Crawdads Sings

The year is 1965.

Kya cooked some food for herself and then went to the marsh in a white dress. The next morning, Kya went to meet Chase. She wore a white blouse to look like a normal girl. Chase took the boat to Point Beach, and asked Kya if she wants to walk. She agreed. They were both tall and tan. Chase chose to work for his dad instead of going to college. Kya just wanted to fill the emptiness inside her. Chase found a shell and Kya gave its Latin name and explained why it occurs here in nature. Chase was surprised because Kya couldn't even spell dog at one point. Chase brought his picnic basket, and Kya had her first soft drink ever. Chase played the harmonica, and they talked about the sea. Chase sat closer to her and then kissed her. Then he took off her blouse and went on top of her. Kya was put off by this and got herself away from under him. When he touched her face, she stood up. She thought she was ready for this, but now knew she's not. The two were silent for a while, then Chase reached for her hand, but she pulled her hand away. Chase apologized and said he just take her to her boat. She walked toward the woods, then ran. She was guided by blackbirds, and she was sobbing. Kya felt ashamed and sad. She wanted to be with someone and to be wanted, but it backfired on her. She wasn't sure if she wanted Chase to come apologize to her but then walked to her boat.

It sounds like she was ashamed of her needs and wants which is what happens to neglected children. When parents neglect children, it sends the message to the child that he or she isn't important. This leads kids to seek attention in the wrong places when they become teens so they can get their needs met.

Chapter Twenty-Four Summary of Where the Crawdads Sings

Kya hadn't seen Chase in ten days but then saw him getting reading for a picnic with friends. She wanted to get away on her boat but something drew her to him, and she know this was irrational. She decided to go after him. They made eye contact, and Kya sped off on her boat because she was shy. Then, ten minutes later she saw Chase by himself, and he told her he wants to show her the fire tower. Chase told her to go to Barkley Cove, to a forest she's never been to before, and the area was a swamp. This land was higher than the marsh. Chase took her to the fire tower, and they saw another young man and woman there. Chase apologized to her again. Kya gave him a necklace that she made out of the shell they found during their picnic. Chase asked Kya to take her to her house, and Kya made the excuse that it's far. Kya decided to show him her house. Chase asked her how long she has lived here alone, and she said ten years. Chase thought it was cool that she doesn't have parents telling her what to do. Kya said there's nothing to see in her shack. Chase had never see a house like Kya's. It was like a house from the 20's with no electricity and no running water. Kya didn't think she had any snacks to offer her guest. Chase held her while they stood in her house and told her even the boys would have been afraid to live in a place like this alone. Kya asks him directly what he wants with her, and he just says he wants to get to know her. Chase is curious about her self-reliance and thinks she's beautiful. He asked to come back the next day and Kya said yes. She was hopeful that something good might come from this potential relationship.

Chapter Twenty-Five Summary of Where the Crawdads Sings

The year is 1969.

Chase's mom came to Ed's office. Her name is Patti Love Andrews. Ed offered her coffee, but she didn't want any and asked about the lab report and leads. Patti doesn't think Chase's death was an accident and Ed agrees, but says there's nothing definitive yet. Patti talked about the shell necklace Chase had around his neck when he died. Ed asked if someone significant made the necklace for him. Patti didn't want to admit that her son was in touch with one of the trashy marsh people. Patti could feel that the Marsh Girl was somehow involved with the death of her son. Chase was talking to the Marsh Girl a year before he got married and some think after he got married as well. Chase married Pearl, and Patti believes that the Marsh Girl took the necklace back. When Patti left, Ed and Joe couldn't understand why Clark, aka Kya, would have taken the necklace off him if people would suspect she's the killer. Plus, Ed doesn't think a girl could have pushed an athlete like Chase. Joe and Ed decide to visit Kya to question her. The two of them looked for a shell necklace under the fire tower, but didn't find one. As Ed and Joe got lost on the way to Kya's shack, they ran into a shack full of naked potheads. Ed and Joe tried to talk to her for a few days, but no one was home. They decide they may need a warrant.

Chapter Twenty-Six Summary of Where the Crawdads Sings

Chase saw Kya almost every day for a few weeks and took her to places she's never been to before. Kya felt she was giving a little of herself away to be a part of someone else's life. When Chase was gone for the afternoon, Kya didn't feel alone. Then she saw Tate when she was driving her boat and she'd seen him several times over the past years. She assumed he was home from college. She took her boat in the direction she came from after watching him for a while.

The following day, Kya and Chase took a cruise along the coast. Chase played a song on his harmonica. For many weeks, the two of them spent time on the beach and held hands. Chase kissed her one night, and he held her as they were wrapped in a blanket by the campfire.

A few days after this, Tate decides to visit Kya for the first time in five years. He realized he can't live without her and none of the other girls compare. Tate was in grad school and on track to finish his PhD in three years. Tate saw Kya's boat zooming east and Chase's boat coming towards her. He saw the two of them kiss. Tate thought Kya knew nothing about Chase's town life, and he knew he didn't have the moral right to say anything to her since he hadn't treated her better. He didn't even have courage to properly break up with her a few years back. Tate decided to turn back and help his dad instead.

A few days from there, Kya got tired of waiting for Chase and decided to pack some food and go to her log cabin where she was liberated from having to wait for anyone. She wanted some more books so decided to go to the library and get some textbooks. She read an article about imposter male bullfrogs who were called "sneaky fuckers." She remembered how her Mom taught her sister than unworthy guys make a lot of noise just like the alpha male bullfrogs who croak loudly. Chase wanted to see her on a specific day after she had been gone for three days. Chase made some advances on her at the beach, but Kya said she wasn't ready yet. Chase mentioned that he was falling in love with her, and she didn't know yet how she felt about him. Kya knows that stars and time aren't fixed but always move. Objects fall into the space-time folds. Kya ran into Chase's parents at the Piggly Wiggly the next morning, and later asked Chase when she will get to meet his parents. He said soon. Kya always resisted Chase's moves and the closest they got was just lying naked in a boat but no further. There were a lot of rumors about them in town.

Chapter Twenty-Seven Summary of Where the Crawdads Sings

The year is 1966.
Chase and Kya had been together for a year now.
Chase began talking to Kya about getting married and
building a house. Kya was in disbelief but really
wanted to be part of a family. Kya didn't know if she
felt the kind of love toward Chase that a wife has for
her husband. Chase wanted to take Kya to Asheville to
go to a store, but Kya was a bit scared of large towns
and people. It would be a two day trip. A few days
later, Kya rode in Chase's truck to Asheville. Kya
looked at the land that once belonged to her great-
grandparents. Chase checked them into a motel.
Chase made love to her for the first time there. A few
weeks later, the two of them were back at Kya's
shack. Kya wanted to meet Chase's family at the
Christmas dinner and wanted to go to the dance club
with him, but he made a bunch of excuses about how
she wouldn't enjoy any of that. Kya ended up being
alone for Christmas.

Four days after Christmas, Chase still hadn't showed up at her house. She imagines he was having fun with friends or was at those dance parties he said he didn't like. She heard a boat and thought Chase was here, but it was Tate! She began to throw rocks at him. Tate said he knows she's with Chase, and Kya says he has no right to talk to her about her personal life. She threw little rocks at his face and said she never wants to see him. Tate tells her that Chase goes after other women too. Kya blames Tate for leaving her and says he's worse than Chase. Tate says he won't bother her anymore and apologizes to her. Tate asked if she was doing fine, and she said yes. He brought her a feather. She took it but didn't thank him. Tate apologized to her again and said that leaving her was his biggest mistake. Tate asked for forgiveness, but Kya said nothing. She looked at the lagoon to see if Chase was coming. Tate saw Chase dancing with different women at the dance in Barkley Cove. It seems that Chase was too embarrassed to take Kya with him because it would harm his reputation.

Sometime later, Kya ran outside because she thought Chase was here, but it was Tate. Tate noticed that Kya had a collection grand enough for a natural history museum. Tate told her to publish her collection in a book because it was more detailed than the current books in print on shells and animals in the marsh. Kya agreed to give him a few samples of her collection and they both realized that one of the samples was the first feather Chase gave her. They looked into each other's eyes, and Tate asked her if she can forgive him. Kya said she can't believe him again. Tate left and Kya went to wait for Chase.

Chase came to Kya a week after Christmas. He said they would spend New Year's Day together. They made love and cuddled near the stove. Chase played his harmonica.

Chapter Twenty-Eight Summary of Where the Crawdads Sings

It's 1969.

Joe and Ed went to a bar, and women weren't allowed there. A bunch of fisherman started asking Joe and Ed questions about Chase's case. A member of the shrimper crew, Hal Miller, wanted to speak to Ed. Hal revealed to Ed that he saw the Marsh Girl in the bay when Chase died. Ed said that he will ask him and Allen Hunt, a guy in his crew, to make a statement about what they saw. Ed told Joe what Hal told him. Joe was hoping to get a warrant from court so he can search Kya's residence.

Chapter Twenty-Nine Summary of Where the Crawdads Sings

It's 1969.

Chase visited Kya often, and she wanted to bake Chase a caramel cake. She ran into Chase near the market. He had his arms around a blond, skinny girl but dropped them when he saw Kya. He awkwardly introduced his friends to her. Chase told her he'd see her on Sunday. Kya saw the truancy lady, Mrs. Culpepper, at the market. She bought a newspaper and found out that a science facility was being built in Sea Oaks. Then she saw an announcement in the paper that Chase was marrying another girl. It was the girl who always wears pears and is part of his group of friends. Kya was shocked. She began to cry, and when she saw Chase's boat approaching, she ran into the woods before he saw her. She fed the gulls French bread when he left.

Chapter Thirty Summary of Where the Crawdads Sings

It's 1967.

Kya went to the waters in her boat and felt like being moved by the most powerful currents to numb her emotional pain. Kya no longer avoided the strong currents of the sea. She was no longer afraid of strong currents. Kya felt like she was sentenced to a life of loneliness. Her boat was full of water now, and she was drenched in water. Kya was heartbroken that she's been rejected her whole life.

My question to her is: How has she rejecting herself in life? Everything we experience is a result of how we feel about ourselves and how we treat ourselves. Once we accept ourselves, other people will too.

Kya felt like she fell for the wrong guy just like Mom did. Kya noticed a beautiful collection of shells on the sand. She decided to collect the rare shells. Kya trusted nature.

Chapter Thirty- One Summary of Where the Crawdads Sings

The year is 1968.
Kya usually only got bulk mail, but she opened the mail box and saw an advance copy of her own book. It's been over a year since Chase got engaged to Pearl. The editor, Mr. Robert Foster, said her book would be published soon because her information on shells was complete. She got an advance payment and her book would appear in bookstores in the south soon. Kya wanted to write a letter to Tate to thank him for helping her get published but didn't feel that a thank you note was enough. She would no longer have to pick mussels to make her living. She did write the note saying to come visit if he's ever near. Kya's house got a major makeover. She called in a repairman named Jerry.
One day Jumpin' told Kya that developers wanted to drain the marsh. Kya had no idea if she was a squatter or if she owned the land she was on. Kya went to the Barkley Cove courthouse and found out her grandpa had bought the land she was on. She was told to pay back taxes to keep the land. The tax she had to pay for forty years was only eight hundred dollars because her house was in the wasteland category. That deed covered three hundred acres of land!
Kya got a letter from Tate, and he came to visit her. He squeezed Kya's hand to thank her for signing a copy of Kya's book for him. Tate began to leave, and just as he was getting on his boat, he told Kya not to hide from him when she sees him working at the lab. He says they can go explore the marsh. She thought about being Tate's friend or even his colleague.

Kya went to see Jumpin' and handed him her book. She thanked him for all he had done for her over the years. Jumpin' was speechless for the first time. Kya continued to buy supplies from him, and he put her book in the window of his store like a dad would.

Chapter Thirty- Two Summary of Where the Crawdads Sings

It's 1969.

Deputy Joe said that when he went to look for Kya at Jumpin's shop, two reliable sources told him that she was not in town when Chase died. Joe found out from Jumpin' and Dr. Tate Walker that Kya was in Greenville on the night Chase died. Tate said he showed her how to get a bus ticket to Greenville. Kya's alibi is that she was in Greenville because the publishing company invited her and covered all her expenses. Joe also found out that Tate taught Kya to read. Joe said to will be easy to check if she really was in Greenville for two days. Miss Pansy Price then came in to Ed's office and said she and her co-workers saw Kya get on the bus on October 28th and she didn't come back until the 30th. Joe and Ed decide to check the bus schedule to see if her trip to Greenville by bus was even feasible. It turns out it was feasible.

Chapter Thirty- Three Summary of Where the Crawdads Sings

It was 1968.Kya was painting with her watercolors. She already had a book on seabirds and was now working on a guide to mushrooms. She saw a red pickup truck outside her shack. A military guy got out of the truck and knocked on her door. This military man was Kya's brother, Jodie! She recognized him from his scar. Kya had a flashback to a domestic violence scene which explained how Jodie got that scar when he was a kid. It was Kya's dream to see Jodie and her mom. She realized in that moment that Mom left because Dad hit her with a poker in the chest and she bled. Kya welcomed her brother in shyly. She made coffee for him. Jodie would stay in the army for two more months because they paid for his college degree in Georgia Tech. Jodie apologized for leaving Kya with a monster and didn't expect her to forgive him. Jodie talked about how he survived over the years. Jodie's eyes didn't change. Kya said her relationship with Dad was good for a while until he went back to drinking. He also told her that he just found out Mom passed away two years ago. Jodie didn't know what happened to the rest of their siblings. Mom's sister Rosemary said Mom was ill both in the head and physically and went back to New Orleans. Mom didn't come back because Dad threatened to beat his kids if she did. Mom's death was like her life, silent and dark. Jodie presented Kya with Mom's paintings of the family while she was in New Orleans. Kya looked at her siblings' eyes. Kya saw a painting of her and Tate as toddlers. Kya forgives her mother for leaving, but she can't comprehend why she never came back to see her or at least write more letters. She touched Jodie's arm and said this is the happiest and saddest day of her life. Jodie and Kya went on a boat ride and picnic. Jodie told Kya about her siblings. Kya didn't remember her siblings at all. Kya cooked a southern meal, and Jodie said he would stay for a few days. He also told her he would get a job in Atlanta so he can see her as much as possible. Tate came up a lot in the conversation as the two of them talked. Jodie told Kya to give Tate another chance if she still loves him. Jodie gave Kya his address and phone number before he left. He pulled her closer to him and she cried on him.

Chapter Thirty- Four Summary of Where the Crawdads Sings

It's 1969.
The sheriff and deputy now have a search warrant and look through Kya's home when she's not there. Joe finds a red had that has the same fibers as Chase's jean jacket have. They take the hat in for testing and leave Kya's shack.

Chapter Thirty- Five Summary of Where the Crawdads Sings

It's July of 1969.
Kya published another book, this time on seacoast birds. It's been seven months since Jodie visited Kya. When Kya went to look for mushrooms, she found a milk carton with a note from Tate and a compass. Tate said the compass belonged to his grandpa, but she may need it. Kya still hid from Tate when he did research in the marsh. A few mornings later, Kya saw Tate's boat and recited a poem.

Chapter Thirty- Six Summary of Where the Crawdads Sings

Kya's hat fibers matched the fibers on Chase's jacket. Joe said they need to find a better motive, but she can be brought in and questioned. Joe and Ed think about trapping her but know it would be wrong. A retired mechanic, Rodney Horn, comes into Ed's office and tells them what he saw in Cypress Cove on August 30th. After he left, Joe believed that they now have a motive.

Chapter Thirty- Seven Summary of Where the Crawdads Sings

Kya waved at Jumpin,' but he didn't wave back. Police boats chased her, and she was arrested for murdering Chase.

Chapter Thirty- Eight Summary of Where the Crawdads Sings

The year is 1970.
Kya was led to her lawyer, Tom Milton. She was in handcuffs. It was February 25th. Tom told Kya that things would be fine. Kya never looked at her lawyer and never answered questions. The lawyer brought her a book about shells, and she started listening to him a bit more. Villagers started to take their seats in the courtroom which created a restless feeling. Barkley Cove was the first place that was settled in North Carolina. Hank Jones is the bailiff and Miss Henrietta Jones is his daughter. Mr. Eric Chastain is the prosecution attorney. Harold Sims is the judge. The judge announced that Catherine Clark is being charged with first degree murder. Sunday Justice, the courthouse cat, jumped on the judge's bench. The jury was selected by noon. Kya recognized a few people in the jury. The judge announced a lunch recess.

Chapter Thirty- Nine Summary of Where the Crawdads Sings

It's 1969.

Kya went to a peninsula called Cypress Cove. It's been over a month since Tate gave Kya the compass. Kya heard a voice, and realized it was Chase. He called her his marsh girl. Chase apologized to Kya for not marrying her and said she loves him. She said she doesn't think she ever loved him. Chase harassed her and kicked her. He may have raped her. Kya kicked him in the groin and back. Then she ran to her boat and took off.

Chapter Forty Summary of Where the Crawdads Sings

It's 1970.
Judge Sims told Eric Chastain to call his first witness. He called Rodney Horn. Kya recognized him. Rodney said he saw Miss Clark kicking Chase and heard her say that if he bothers her, she'll kill him. Tom went to the stand and asked Rodney if the screaming from the woods sounded like Miss Clark was defending herself, and Rodney said it was possible.

Chapter Forty-One Summary of Where the Crawdads Sings

The year is 1969.

Kya drove home and watched out for Chase. She got home with a swollen eye, and she realized Chase still wore her shell necklace. Kya knew the fishermen who saw them fighting wouldn't defend her, and the law was on Chase's side. Kya walked to the reading cabin. Tate and his dad had fixed up that reading cabin. She listened for predators and Chase just outside the cabin. Kya was ashamed because she had lots of cuts and believed she brought this situation on her own. She slept in Tate's cabin bed. In the morning, Kya ate breakfast and realized why Mom couldn't come home; because Mad beat her. Kya faced the same situation as her Mom because she couldn't come home either now. Kya promised herself to never live a life where she's constantly afraid of being beaten. Kya didn't want anyone to see her beaten face. Female praying mantis eat their lovers, and Kya saw one doing this. Kya listened to the sound of birds and went to an area Chase doesn't know of.

Chapter Forty-Two Summary of Where the Crawdads Sings

It's 1970.
Kya sat in a jail cell. Kya couldn't be bailed out because she tried to run from the cops the day they arrested her. Kya recalled a poem. The only other prisoners were two guys who caused trouble with their spitting contest. Kya was not afraid to die, but she couldn't imagine someone planning someone's death. Kya couldn't sleep.

Chapter Forty-Three Summary of Where the Crawdads Sings

It's 1969.

In September Kya received a letter from her publisher inviting her to an all-expenses paid trip to Greenville. Kya saw Tate on the marsh and wanted to steer her boat away from him so he couldn't see her bruised face. It was too late because Tate had seen her and wanted to show her his microscope. Kya saw amoebas and thought they were beautiful. Tate made coffee for Kya and asked what happened to her face. Kya lied to him and said a door hit her. Tate wondered if Chase hit her, but changed the subject because he could see she was uneasy. He asked her about a new book, and she said she's almost done with her book on mushrooms. She mentioned the invitation she got to meet her publisher in Greenville. Tate told her to take the bus to get there. Kya said she had to leave. Just before she left, Tate threw his cap to her and they tossed it back and forth to each other playfully. Kya didn't want to fall in love with him again. Kya went to feed the gulls, and saw Chase on his boat, racing toward her shack. Kya was glad she wasn't home. She hid from Chase on her boat in the swells. She rode her boat back to her shack in the dark, and slept next to the gulls outside. Kya wanted an escape from living in fear. She wanted peace.

Chapter Forty-Four Summary of Where the Crawdads Sings

It's 1970.

Kya knew that if she had support in her life she wouldn't be in jail; she would be on stable ground. She refused to see Tate when he visited her in jail, and she realized that jail closed her heart. Kya had even less trust in people when she was vulnerable. Kya didn't want to call her brother from jail because she was ashamed. Kya couldn't focus on reading so she looked at pictures of shells. Kya's lawyer came to visit her and told her to plead guilty to manslaughter, but Kya disagreed. The lawyer wanted her to avoid life in prison. When Kya was taken back to her cell by Jacob, the guard, she got a package from Jumpin'. Sunday Justice came to visit Kya in her cell. The cat sat on her lap and purred. Kya felt accepted. The cat helped Kya fall asleep and slept next to her. The next morning, Kya told Jacob to let Sunday Justice into her cell whenever he wants. Jacob brought Kya her dinner at the end of the day and brought the cat to her. Kya wasn't hungry although the food was better than what she had been eating her whole life. She gave the chicken to Sunday Justice and later fell asleep with the cat.

Tate came to visit Kya and this time Kya consented to seeing him. Tate said she has a good lawyer and will be out of jail soon. Kya tells him to forget her. Tate said he will come to court every day and feed the gulls. Kya tells him she doesn't ever want to be close to anyone anymore. She thanks him for coming but says she can't think about her future while in jail. She tells him that maybe one day they can be friends.

Chapter Forty-Five Summary of Where the Crawdads Sings

Kya focused on the trees outside when she goes to court on Monday. She sees Tate sitting with Jumpin' and Mabel. Kya felt stronger when she saw them there. Dr. Steward Cone was a coroner and a witness. No alcohol was found in Chase's body. Chase didn't wear a shell necklace when he was examined by Steward. There was no evidence to show that Chase was pushed because there were no bruises from a push on his body, and the red fibers on his jacket could have been there for years. There was no evidence found that Kya had been with Chase the night he died. The court was dismissed for lunch. Kya still hadn't called her brother to come visit her in jail.

Chapter Forty-Six Summary of Where the Crawdads Sings

The year is 1969.
Kya got to Jumpin' to ask him about the bus schedule. She wanted to meet her editor. Kya told Jumpin' she might go to see her editor in Greenville. Kya admitted to Jumpin' that Chase beat her, and told him not to tell anyone. Kya explained to him that the law would not be on her side if she told someone, and she would be humiliated. Jumpin' told her to let her know when she's going out of town so he can be sure she's safe.

Chapter Forty-Seven Summary of Where the Crawdads Sings

Kya's lawyer was in the witness box and said the tide can wipe out footprints when the water rises. Ed said that if footprints are absent, it doesn't mean a crime wasn't committed. It doesn't mean they were wiped clean. Tom showed there's no evidence Kya was up at the fire tower the day Chase died. He also had Ed read a request that Ed wrote to the U.S. Forest Service to fix the dangerous grates on the fire tower. The request was submitted three months before Chase died.

Chapter Forty-Eight Summary of Where the Crawdads Sings

It's October 28th, 1969.
Kya got on the bus headed for Greenville after telling Jumpin' she's leaving. When Kya came back two days later and went to see Jumpin', he told her Chase died. He also said there were no footprints. Jumpin' told Kya about the funeral. He was secretly glad Kya was out of town or people would think she killed him.

Chapter Forty-Nine Summary of Where the Crawdads Sings

Mr. Larry Price, the bus driver, testified that he saw someone on his bus who could have been a woman disguised as a man. This person was about the same height as Miss Clark. Mr. Price said the bus was twenty-five minutes late when it got to Barkley Cove. Eric called Mr. John King, the bus driver who drove a bus to Greenville in the morning, on October 30th. Mr. King said Kya wasn't on the bus at 2:30 in the morning, but there was an old lady on the bus. Tom questioned him as well and Mr. King, and confirmed that he did not see Kya on his bus that night.

Chapter Fifty Summary of Where the Crawdads Sings

It's 1970.

Kya is in court and sees Jodie. She is ashamed. Mrs. Sam Andrews, aka Patti Love, was called to the stand. She's the mother of Chase. Patti Love is obsessed over how she looks, and says Chase wore the shell necklace all the time. Eric presented the court with a leather journal which Kya once gave to Chase as a gift. Patti Love said Chase got the journal from Miss Clark as a gift. Patti Love was embarrassed that her son was with the Marsh Girl. There was a picture in the journal of Chase and Kya in the fire tower. The picture showed Kya gifting the shell necklace to Chase. Patti Love realized she didn't know her son at all.

Chapter Fifty-One Summary of Where the Crawdads Sings

The year is 1970.
Kya noticed that alpha males don't need to speak loudly or wear bright ties. Another witness was called to the stand. It was Hal Miller who was a part of Tim O'Neal's shrimp crew. Hall said he saw Miss Clark, but he wasn't sure it was her. It was dark and the moon wasn't out. The boat he saw in the water had no lights on. Hal couldn't even see what clothes she wore so how can he be sure it was Miss Clark?

Chapter Fifty-Two Summary of Where the Crawdads Sings

It's 1970.
Sarah Singletary, the store clerk at the Piggly Wiggly, testified and said she saw Miss Clark get on the bus at two-thirty on October 28th and get off at one-sixteen on October 30th.
The owner of the Three Mountains Motel, Lang Furlough, also testified and said Miss Clark was in her room until October 30th and never left the hotel room.

Scupper finally came to court. He realized his son, Tate, loved Kya his whole life. Scupper was ashamed when he realized he was biased against Kya because she lived in a marsh. Scupper decided to support his son by going to court, and Tate got emotional. Robert Foster was called to the stand and said he was her editor. He confirmed that she was in Greenville for those two days, and he drove her to her hotel at 9:55 on October 29th. Kya remembered that the fancy diner couldn't even compare to her picnic with Tate. She watched a flock of birds soaring in the sky during her picnic which was better than her diner in Greenville. Kya suddenly felt like she couldn't breathe, and Tom asked for a short recess. Kya didn't want to sit through the trial anymore, but her lawyer says she has to by law. When court was back in session, Tom asked Ed whether it was feasible timewise for Miss Clark to kill Chase and then take the bus to Greenville, back to her hotel the same night she supposedly killed Chase. Sheriff Ed said it would have been very tight timewise, but Tom said she would have needed an extra twenty minutes to kill Chase and get back to the hotel in Greenville, Three Mountains Hotel. The sheriff also had no evidence that there was a strong riptide that would have taken Kya to the fire tower faster.

Chapter Fifty-Three Summary of Where the Crawdads Sings

It's 1970.

Tim O'Neal, the shrimping operator, was called to the stand. He was the last witness and said he didn't see Miss Clark that night. The boat he saw could have been anyone's boat since she had a common boat type.

Eric stood up to present his closing statement to the jury, and then Tom presented his closing statement. Tom said to judge the case upon the facts, and that the Marsh Girl should be treated fairly. Kya also realized there's no evidence to prove she's guilty, and there wasn't even evidence to prove that this is a murder case.

Chapter Fifty-Four Summary of Where the Crawdads Sings

It's 1970.
Tom went to see Kya and prepare appeal documents. Everyone was waiting for the jury to come up with a verdict. Tate told Tom to tell Kya that they are all here for her and can sit with her. Kya only saw her lawyer Tom. The people of color had to wait outside for the verdict. Kya realized she didn't really know the meaning to loneliness till she got to prison. Kya realized she can't live without the marsh. Kya new there was prejudice against her.
The jury wanted to see the record of bus drivers' testimonies. By four o'clock, the jury decided on a verdict, and everyone went back to court. Tate watched Kya's face. Everyone was breathless as the defendant was asked to read the verdict. Miss Jones, who was the court recorder, read the verdict. Kya was found not guilty! The judge said she's free to go and apologized that she had to be in jail for two months. He also thanked the jury for their time. Some people didn't know why she was let free, but one can only get tired once in a murder trial. Kya's support circled embraced her, and her brother asked if she wanted him to drive her home. She agreed. Kya thanked a few people on her way out.

Chapter Fifty-Five Summary of Where the Crawdads Sings

It's 1970.

Jodie drove Kya home as her mind raced. Kya ran up to the beach and birds, and then went home to make tea. Jodie asks to stay with Kya for a few days. Kya says she's gotten used to living alone. Kya went outside and Jodie made food. Then he drove his truck near the beach and Kya went home. She wasn't hungry and began painting grasses. She didn't know why she was angry. She wanted a cat because the one at court accepted her as she is. The next morning, Kya made breakfast and went to the channel.

In the distance, Kya saw Tate's boat being chased by a sheriff's and deputy's boat. Kya was confused and thought maybe Tate was accused on a crime too. Kya finally realized that the only reason she survived in the marsh was because of Tate. When she caught glimpses on him, it's like she was being filled with love but never shared it. Kya took her boat across the marsh.

Chapter Fifty-Six Summary of Where the Crawdads Sings

It's 1970.

Tate found out that his dad passed away, and he went to the cemetery. Tate was angry at his dad for thinking about Kya even during the funeral. He regretted not spending more time with him. His mother and sister were also buried there. Tate went back to town on his truck. Tate noticed a brown feather on the seat of his cabin cruiser. Tate didn't think Kya was here. He drove the boat to Kya's shack and saw her standing on the porch. Tate held Kya and told her he loves her. Kya told him she's always loved him even when he was a kid. Tate said that he wants to know that her days of running away are over and that she can love without fear. They walked through the woods.

Chapter Fifty-Seven Summary of Where the Crawdads Sings

The two of them slept on the beach, and then Tate moved in with Kya the next day. Tate asked her if she will marry him, and Kya said they are married like geese are. They liked to collect feathers and swim naked in the moonlight. Kya was offered a job by a lab, but she decided to write books instead. The two of them hired someone to build a lab and a studio for them. They also built an additional bedroom and bathroom in their home. Kya invited her brother and his wife over to explore the marsh. Kya never came to Barkley Cove anymore. Kya became a living legend over the years and lived with Tate in the marsh. It was never discovered who killed Chase, and people agreed Kya shouldn't have been arrested. Kya was pretty content with her life. Kya was confident that Tate wouldn't leave her. Kya never completely healed from how she had been treated in the past. Tate came back from a trip once and said Jumpin' passed away. She cried. Kya didn't go to the funeral but brought blackberry jam to Mabel's house and said her condolences to Jumpin' in her own way. Jodie and his wife, Libby, brought their kids to Kya's house and it was full of love and joy.

There were many changed at Barkley Cove over the years. Jumpin's shop was now a marina. It had a lot more coffee shops and touristy places. People of all colors and both genders could now go to the beer hall. Tate kept his lab job, and Kya wrote more books. The University of North Carolina gave her an honorary doctorate. Kya and Tate weren't able to have kids, but that brought them closer together. Kya felt connected to the earth when she walked alone on the beach. Tate made Kya believe in human love, and it wasn't just about passing on genes to future generations. Tate found Kya dead in a lagoon at age sixty-four. He cried. Tate had to ask for permission to bury her under at oak. Lots of people came to her funeral to pay their respects. Tate found a lot of boxes at home which were full of Kya's stuff. Tate found the property deed. Tate didn't find a will. He found a box full of poems by Amanda Hamilton. Tate realized Amanda Hamilton was Kya's pen name. Tate read one of her poems out loud. Tate also found the necklace which Kya took from Chase when he died. Tate remembered how Kya took night buses and pushed Chase off the fire tower and nature protected her secret. Tate burned Kya's poems in the woodstove and the rawhide from the shell. He dropped the shell on the sand at around dusk. The gulls called, and Tate watched fireflies as it got dark.

Setting of Where the Crawdads Sing

The entire story takes place in North Carolina. Most of it takes place in Kya's shack and at the marsh. The reading cabin is an abandoned shack to which Kya escaped to when she felt threatened or unsafe. There is also Colored Town where Jumpin' and his family lived. Barkley Cove is a place full of shows and businesses. Kya went there for supplies. Jumpin's shop was there and so is the Piggly Wiggly market. The fire tower is where Chase Andrews died. Point Beach was the place Kya watched people and picked up shells, but never interacted with the people there until she met Chase there. Greenville is a place Kya's dad wanted to take her to because part of it belonged to her great-grandparents. She also stayed at a motel with Chase in Greenville, and it's also the place she met her publisher at.

Main and Secondary Character List of Where the Crawdads Sing

Main Characters

Kya- the main character and protagonist of the novel. Also known as Miss Catherine Danielle Clark or The Marsh Girl. She is shy and attentive.

Jodie- Kya's brother and her only remaining family. He left at around age eleven, but reunited with Kya late.

Tate Walker- Her boyfriend turned husband. He taught her to read and in the long run was the only person really there for her in life. He helped Kya publish her first book.

Chase Andrews- A popular guy Kya once dated and was accused of murdering. He once asked Kya to marry her, but he married someone else.

Jumpin'- He was also known as Mister Jake. He was like a father to Kya especially after her real dad disappear. He owned a gas station and shop.

Secondary Characters

Kya's mother and father- Maria and Jake. Both left Kya to fend on her own.

Kya's three other siblings- Kya doesn't even remember what they look like until she sees a painting of them.

Tom Milton- Kya's lawyer.

Miss Pansy Price- A landowner Chase bumps into once.

Miss Arial- Kya's second grade teacher. Kya only attended one day of school.

Mrs. Singletary- The cashier at the Piggly Wiggly. She questioned why Kya wasn't at school and taught her to count money. She also helped her pay for groceries.

Benji Mason and Steve Long- The two boys who found Chase's body at the bottom of the fire tower.

Mrs. Culpepper- The truancy lady.

Sheriff Ed Jackson- The town's sheriff.

Dr. Vern Murphy- The town physician who examined the dead body.

Chase's friends- Kya had different nick names for them such as girl who wears pearls and tall skinny blond. They never became Kya's friends.

Joe Purdue- A deputy.

Sheriff Jackson- A sheriff who worked on the murder case.

Scupper- Tate's father.

Mr. Lane- Worked at Sing Oil.

Mrs. Teresa White- The mother of a little girl who once reached out to Kya. Teresa told her daughter that Kya looks dirty. Teresa later served on the jury for Chase's murder.

Mabel- Jumpin's wife. She provided supplies and support for Kya.

Patti Love Andrews- Chase's mom. Also known as Mrs. Sam Andrews.

Hal Miller and Allen Hunt- Guys on the shrimp crew.

Girl who always wears pears- The girl Chase married.

Mr. Robert Foster- Kya's editor. He testified in court.

Jerry- The repair guy who fixed Kya's shack.

Rodney Horn- A retired mechanic.

Hank Jones- The bailiff.

Miss Henrietta Jones- The bailiff's daughter.

Mr. Eric Chastain- The prosecution attorney.

Sunday Justice- The courthouse cat. He gave Kya unconditional love.

Mr. John King- The bus driver who was questioned in court.

Mr. Larry Price- Another bus driver.

Tim O'Neal- The shrimping operator.

Miss Jones- The court recorder who read the verdict.

Libby- Jodie's wife. They also have kids later on.

Dr. Steward Cone- The coroner and witness.

Lang Furlough- Owner of the Three Mountains Hotel.

Themes in Where the Crawdads Sing

Coming of age- This novel tells a story about how a girl grew up, mostly on her own.

Death- A lot of people and creatures either passed away or were killed in this novel.

Companionship as a type of salvation- Who knows if Kya would have survived the rest of her life is she didn't accept Tate. She admitted by the end of the novel that he's the reason she liked to ride her boat through the marsh. She caught glimpses of him and it gave her peace and meaning.

Need to escape- Kya felt the need to escape conventions and people. The marsh and nature are her forms of escape. She never fully integrated into mainstream society.

Betrayal and heartbreak- Kya had dealt with a lot of heartbreak in her life. Her first heartbreak was when her mother left. She was heartbroken when Tate didn't visit her and when Chase betrayed her. Dealing with prejudice and loss is a common experience for Kya.

Loneliness and Isolation- Kya faced varying degrees of loneliness throughout her life. The worst loneliness was when she was locked behind bars. She never found a group of people she belonged to. Her family was the wildlife and nature. The only person who eased her loneliness in the long term was Tate. She has been abandoned and isolated for most of her life and was forced to raise herself.

Oppression- There was a lot of female oppression and racism throughout the story. It took place in a time when people weren't equal. Women were called their husband's name as in the case of Mrs. Sam Andrews, and people of color were segregated. If was less common for women to hold leadership roles. Kya faced a lot of prejudice because she was poor and a nonconformist.

Survival, Self-Reliance, and Heroism- Kya was a survivor her whole life and had to perform heroic feats just to survive. At just seven, she had to learn to drive a boat, fish, and make a living. She had to count money and make business deals. She also had to cook and clean. She learned how to avoid predator and danger. She practiced reading and eventually was more educated than the teachers which is a heroic feat considering she had only been to school for one day. Kya relied on herself and nature for most of her life.

Symbols and Motifs in Where the Crawdads Sing

Shells- This is a motif that represents secrets. They are the best at keeping secrets in the natural world. Chase's shell necklace is symbolic because his death later proved to be the best kept secret. Shells are tied to the theme of death.

Eyes- This is another motif. The eyes of the fish, Kya's mother, Tate, Chase, and the little girl who reached out to Kya really caught Kya's attention. She tends to pay attention to eyes.

Water- Water symbolizes movement and flow. When the sea is turbulent, Kya's life is also turbulent. A turbulent sea may symbolize troubles ahead.

Nature- This is another motif related to the themes of need to escape and coming of age. Nature plays a nurturing role in Kya's life, and she also escapes into the wilderness to be who she is. She was raised by the wilderness.

Birds and crawdads- They are guides and symbols of movement. Bird often guided Kya and cheered her up. She was able to tell by their movement if something was up, especially if the crows circled around something. When she was isolated, they embraced her. They are also symbols of freedom because they can soar through the sky freely and Kya felt free with them.

Doves and crows- Doves are a symbol of peace and stability. Crows are a symbol of death.

Sunday Justice- The courthouse cat is a symbol of unconditional acceptance and kindness. Sunday Justice acts like he doesn't care at times, but this is the same characteristic that makes him accepting of others because he doesn't judge them.

Foreshadowing in Where the Crawdads Sing

Throughout the novel, Kya pointed out many examples of insects eating their mates or female animals taking advantage of male ones. These examples foreshadow the murder of Chase.

In the first chapter, the marsh is described as a place which captures people. This symbolizes and foreshadows the traps of life which Kya faced. It also foreshadows death as a type of trap.

Discussion Questions for Where the Crawdads Sing

1. Insects sometimes eat their mates. Frogs sometimes lie and pretend to be an alpha male

by basically standing in the shadows of one. What is an appropriate punishment for a human who mistreats his or her mate?

2. Is it feasible for a six year old girl to survive on her own after being abandoned by parents?
3. Should Kya have gone to school as a child? You she have been better off going to school?
4. Would should a mother do if she lives with an abusive partner?
5. Would Kya have been better off in a foster home?
6. Did the police treat Kya appropriately when they arrested her?
7. Why didn't anyone in the community help Kya when she was growing up? Is it because she pretended to have parents?
8. Is it better to have loved and lost or never to have loved at all?
9. How did nature allow Kya to survive and even thrive?
10. Who was the most influential person in Kya's life?
11. Which person caused her the most pain?
12. Why is it important for people to be integrated in their community?
13. Did Chase deserve to end up the way he did?
14. Was Kya morally wrong?
15. Did Kya have a meaningful and fulfilling life?
16. How does childhood neglect affect a person?

Thank you for reading!

We hope you learned something interesting from this summary.
We care about your reading experience here at Book Nerd and want to provide you with thorough and insightful book guides.
We'd like to give you a virtual high five for reading until the very end. You're a great reader!
Before we part ways, do you mind leaving us a review on Amazon? We would appreciate that greatly, and your support will help us create more book guides in the future.
Thanks again!

Yours Truly,
Book Nerd Team
Don't forget your gift!

https://www.subscribepage.com/2books

ABOUT BOOK NERD

Book Nerd is dedicated to providing readers with thorough and thoughtful summaries.

CPSIA information can be obtained
at www.ICGtesting.com
Printed in the USA
BVHW031308270319
543857BV00001B/27/P